I0101055

LOVE

365

Bree Abbington

Copyright © 2014 Bree Abbington

All rights reserved.

ISBN: 0615968503
ISBN-13 978-0615968506

DEDICATION

To all of the people in my life who have taught me
about what love truly is.

PREFACE

Love takes limitless forms. Love is universal, but love's definition is unique to each person. In each of our lives, we are likely to experience many different types of love. Even the love between the same two individuals will morph and change over time. Love can lift you to new heights, or slam you against the rocks on any given day. Love is one of the strongest of human emotions.

Love – 365 is a celebration of the positive side of love. It contains quotes that span time, and cut across cultural lines. Where the origin is known, the source is cited. Many quotes are attributable to the ageless savant "unknown." These quotes are without citation. I hope you enjoy, and in the end always choose love!

LOVE
365

Falling in love is like jumping off a really tall building. Your head tells you "Idiot, you're going to die." But your heart tells you, "don't worry you can fly."
-Paulo Coelho

Real love doesn't care about body type, model looks, or wallet size. It only cares about what is inside.

A person is only as good as what they love.
-Saul Bellow

Love isn't perfect. It isn't a fairytale or a storybook, and it doesn't always come easy. Love is overcoming obstacles, facing challenges, fighting to be together, holding on, and never letting go. It is a short word, easy to spell, difficult to define, and impossible to live without. Love is work, but most of all, love is realizing that every hour, every minute, every second of it was worth it because you did it together.

-Ritu Ghatourey

Love me when I least deserve it; because that is
when I really need it.
-Swedish proverb

Distance between two hearts is not an obstacle;
rather a beautiful reminder of just how strong
true love can be.

The chance to love and be loved exists no
matter where you are.
-Oprah Winfrey

Piglet: How do you spell love?
Pooh: You don't spell it, you feel it.
-From Winnie the Pooh

When you truly love someone, you give
everything you can and never expect a return.

I do love nothing in the world so much as you.
-William Shakespeare

Everyone says that love hurts, but that is not true. Loneliness hurts. Rejection hurts. Losing someone hurts. Everyone confuses these things with love, but in reality, love is the only thing in that covers up all the pain and makes us feel wonderful again.

"I love you" means that I accept you for the person that you are, and that I do not wish to change you into someone else. It means that I will love you and stand by you even through the worst of times. It means loving you when you are in a bad mood or too tired to do the things I want to do. It means loving your down, not just when you're fun to be with. "I love you" means that I know your deepest secrets and do not judge you for them, asking in return only that you do not judge me for mine. It means that I care enough to fight for what we have and that I love you enough not to let you go.

Find that guy that will pick up every piece of
your shattered heart & put it back together;
keeping one piece for himself, replacing it with a
piece of his heart.

When the power of love overcomes the love of
power, the world will know peace.
-Jimi Hendrix

Everyone says you only fall in love once, but
that's not true, because every time I see you, I
fall in love all over again.

I'm scared of walking out of this room,
and never feeling the rest of my whole life
the way I feel when I'm with you.
-*Dirty Dancing*

Don't forget I'm just a girl, standing in front of a
boy, asking him to love her.
-*Notting Hill*

Love is a promise; love is a souvenir, once given
never forgotten, never let it disappear.
-John Lennon

I really can't picture anyone having a crush on
me.
I can't picture someone thinking about me.
I can't picture someone thinking about me
before they fall asleep.
I can't picture anyone getting butterflies because
I said hi to them, or even just smiled at them.
I can't picture someone smiling at the computer
screen or their cell phones when we are talking.
Why would they even do that?
I'm just me.

You see in all my life I've never found
What I couldn't resist what I couldn't turn down
I could walk away from anyone I ever knew
But I can't walk away from you

I have never let anything have this much control
over me
I work too hard to call my life my own
And I've made myself a world and it's worked so
perfectly
But it's your world now I can't refuse
I've never had so much to lose
Oh I'm shameless
-Garth Brooks,
from *Shameless*

When I saw you I was afraid to meet you. When
I met you I was afraid to kiss you. When I
kissed you I was afraid to love you. Now that I
love you, I am afraid to lose you.

If love is great, and there are no greater things,
then what I feel for you must the greatest.
-Albert Einstein

You come to love not by finding the perfect
person but by seeing an imperfect person
perfectly.

I'll pull the stars down from the heavens to fill
your empty skies.

Love is a great thing, a great good in every way;
it alone lightens what is heavy and leads
smoothly over all roughness.
-Thomas A. Kempis

One day, someone will walk into your life, and
make you see why it never worked out with
anyone else.

You may not be her first, her last, or her only.
She loved before she may love again. But if she
loves you now, what else matters? She's not
perfect – you aren't either, and that the two of
you may never be perfect together but if she can
make you laugh, cause you to think twice, and
admit to being human and making mistakes,
hold onto her and give her the most that you
can. She may not be thinking about you every
second of the day, but she will give you a part of
her that she knows that you can break – her
heart. So don't hurt her, don't change her, don't
analyze and don't expect more than she can give.
Smile when she makes you happy, let her know
when she makes you mad, and miss her when
she's not there.
-Bob Marley

You and I are the best team of all.
You are my best friend and the love of my life,
my heart, my soul, the one I want to be with
each and every day. You are the one I want to
cheer me on through my life. Your arms are the
ones I want to comfort and support me.
I love how when you and I work together we
can do anything.
-Karen Kastyla

If you love something let it go. If it comes back to you it's yours. If it doesn't it never was.

We are all a little weird and life's a little weird, and when we find someone whose weirdness is compatible with ours, we join up with them and fall in mutual weirdness and call it love.
-Dr. Seuss

People build up walls not to keep others out, but to see who cares enough to break them down.

Only love lets us see normal things in an extraordinary way.

Love is a fruit in season at all times, and within reach of very hand.
-Mother Teresa

We go together like copy and paste.

Live life passionately
Love unconditionally
Hope for the best
Laugh your heart out
Cry when wounded and learn from your past
But most of all remember whatever is meant to
be, will eventually find its way to you

The glory of friendship is not the outstretched hand, nor the kindly smile, nor the joy of companionship; it is the spiritual inspiration that comes to one when you discover that someone else believes in you and is willing to trust you with a friendship.
-Ralph Waldo Emerson

Love. If you have it you don't need anything
else, and if you don't have it, it doesn't matter
much what else you have.

To love is to receive a glimpse of heaven.
-Karen Sunde

Love is most weak when there is more doubt
than there is trust, but love is most strong when
you learn to trust even with all the doubts.

Do ordinary things with extraordinary love.
-Mother Teresa

Love is giving someone the power to destroy you, but trusting them not to.

We don't love qualities, we love persons; sometimes by reason of their defects as well as their qualities.
-Jacques Maritain

I love you without knowing how, or when, or from where. I love you straightforwardly, without complexities or pride; so I love you because I know no other way that this: where I do not exist, nor your, so close that your hand on my chest is my hand, so close that your eyes close as I fall asleep.
-Sonnet XVII, Pablo Neruda

If you love someone, tell him or her. Forget about the rules or the fear of looking ridiculous. What is truly ridiculous is passing up on an opportunity to tell someone that your heart is invested in him or her.

To love is nothing.
To be loved is something.
To love and be loved is everything.

Westley and I are joined by the bonds of love.
And you cannot track that, not with a thousand
hounds. And you cannot break it, not with a
thousand swords.
-Robin Wright,
The Princess Bride

True love never dies. It only gets stronger with
time.

A life lived in love will never be dull.

Girl, I live off how you make me feel.
-Marc Anthony

If a guy treats you like his princess, than he
definitely wants to be your prince.

Falling in love with someone isn't always going to be easy. There will be anger, tears, and laughter. It's when you want to be together despite it all. That's when you truly love one another. I'm sure of it.

Cinderella walked on broken glass.
Aurora let a whole lifetime pass.
Belle feel in love with a hideous beast.
Jasmine married a common thief.
Ariel walked on land for love and life.
Snow White barely escaped the knife.
Rapunzel had to find a new dream.
Tiana kissed her prince and turned green.
Mulan left to be a man.
Pocahontas styed to save her land.
It's all about the smiles and tears; because love
means facing your biggest fears!

If what you see by the eye doesn't please you,
then close your eyes and see from the heart.
Because the heart can see beauty and love more
than they eyes can ever wonder.

To love someone deeply gives you strength.
Being loved by someone deeply gives you
courage.
-Lao Tzu

Love is what makes two people sit in the middle
of a bench even if there is plenty of room at
both ends.

To love and be loved is to feel the sun from
both sides.

Love is a friendship set to music.
-Joseph Campbell

I stupidly smile at my phone when I see your
name on the screen.

I realized something I need you, I trust you, I admire you, I want you. And you can be wrong a lot of the time, and we can fight, and get mad at each other, but nothing, nothing in this world can change that. I love you!

I am nothing special, of this I am sure. I am a common man with common thoughts and I've led a common life. There are no monuments dedicated to me and my name will soon be forgotten, but I've loved another with all my heart and soul, and to me, that has always been enough.
-Nicholas Sparks,
The Notebook

Love is a great beautifier.
-Louisa May Alcott

A true love story never ends.

If you can make a woman laugh, you can make
her do anything.
-Marilyn Monroe

Love is about trust.

Any man who can drive safely while kissing a pretty girl is simply not giving the kiss the attention it deserves.
-Albert Einstein

I just want to be your last.

I no longer believed in the idea of soul mates, or love at first sight. But I was beginning to believe that a very few times in your life, if you were lucky, you might meet someone who was exactly right for you. Not because he was perfect, or because you were, but because your combined flaws were arranged in a way that allowed two separate beings to hinge together.
-Lisa Kleypas,
Blue Eyed Devil

Love is patient, love is kind.
It does not envy, it does not boast, it is not
proud.
It is not rude, it is not self-seeking, it is not easily
angered, it keeps no record of wrongs.
Love does not delight in evil but rejoices with
the truth.
It always protects, always trusts, always hopes,
always perseveres.
-The Holy Bible

Love is not about how much you say "I love you" but how much you can prove that it is true.

Nobody has ever measured, not even poets, how much the heart can hold.
-Zelda Fitzgerald

We may love the wrong person, and cry over the wrong person, but one thing is for sure. Mistakes help us find the right person.

The more you give, the more you get back.
That's the way love works.

As love grows in you, beauty grows too. For
love is the beauty of the soul.
-Saint Augustine of Hippo

Forever is a long time. But I wouldn't mind
spending it by your side.

I think if I've learned anything about friendship, it's to hang in, stay connected, fight for them, and let them fight for you. Don't walk away, don't be distracted, don't be too busy or tired, don't take them for granted. Friends are part of the glue that holds life and faith together.
Powerful stuff.
-Jon Katz

"You could have had anything else in the world,
and you asked for me."
She smiled up at him.
Filthy as he was, covered in blood and dirt, he
was the most beautiful thing she'd ever seen.
"But I don't want anything else in the world."
-Cassandra Clare
City of Glass

Somewhere between all our laughs long talks, stupid little fights, and all our lame jokes, I fell in love.

Love is like war; easy to begin but very hard to stop.
-H.L. Mencken

Love is like a butterfly – hold it too tight, you will crush it. Hold it too loose, it will fly.

I but know that I love thee, whatever thou art.
-Thomas Moore

Love is like a lost object. If you search to hard,
you won't find it. But, if you forget about it
momentarily it will show up in the most
unexpected way.

I was enchanted to meet you
-Taylor Swift

If you'll be my soft and sweet,
I'll be your strong and steady.
You'll be my glass of wine,
I'll be your shot of whiskey.
You'll be my sunny day.
I'll be your shade tree. You'll be my
honeysuckle,
I'll be your honeybee.
-Toby Keith

I heard what you said.
I'm not the silly romantic you think.
I don't want the heavens or the shooting stars.
I don't want gemstones or gold. I have those
things already.
I want…a steady hand.
A kind soul.
I want to fall asleep, and wake, knowing my
heart is safe. I want to love, and be loved.
-Shana Abe

Find a heart that will you at your worst, and arms that will hold you at your weakest.

It is a risk to love. What if it doesn't work out?
Ah, but what if it does!
-Peter McWilliams

Love is great and possible, always, but it is very rare to have the feeling that "I want to be with this person forever."

A kiss is lovely trick designed by nature to stop
speech when words become superfluous.

Love is needing someone. Love is putting up
with someone's bad qualities because somehow
complete you.
-Sarah Dessen,
This Lullaby

Love puts the fun in together. The sad in apart.
The home in tomorrow. The joy in my heart.

A man reserves his true and deepest love not for the species of woman in whose company he finds himself electrified and enkindled, but for that one in whose company he may feel tenderly drowsy.
-George Jean Nathan

True believers believers always find each other,
and here we are.
I always knew that you were out there waiting
on me. For me to find my way into your heart.
We can make it work out baby I know it's true.
I can't picture myself with no one but you.
I think I got it right this time.
After all the crazy days I made it through I can't
picture myself with no one but you.
-Keith Urban,
Got it Right this Time

Falling in love is when she falls asleep in your
arms and wakes up in your dreams.

The real lover is the man who can thrill you by
kissing your forehead or smiling into your eyes
or just staring into space.
-Marilyn Monroe.

Love isn't finding someone you can live with.
It's fining someone you can't live without.

Never stop doing little things for others.
Sometimes, those little things occupy the biggest
part of their heart.

Love is like the wind, you can't see it but you
can feel it. -Nicholas Sparks,
A walk to remember

Faith makes all things possible.
Love makes them easy.

I can feel Peeta press his forehead into my temple and he asks, 'So now that you've got me, what are you going to do with me?' I turn into him. 'Put you somewhere you can't get hurt."
-Suzanne Collins,
The Hunger Games

Those who love you are not fooled by mistakes
you have made or dark images you hold about
yourself.
They remember your beauty when you feel ugly:
your wholeness when you are broken;
your innocence when you feel guilty and
your purpose when you feel confused.

Love is not about how much you say "I love you," but how much you prove that it's true.

I love you the same way you learn to ride a bike: scared but reckless.
-Rudy Francisco

Once in a while right in the middle of an ordinary life, love gives us a fairy tale.

Love looks not with the eyes, but with the mind.

Love is a canvas furnished by Nature and
embroidered by imagination.
-Voltaire

Good relationships don't just happen. They
take time, patience, and two people who truly
want to be together.

Every little thing that you do
I'm so in love with you
It just keeps getting better
I wanna spend the rest of my life
With you by my side
Forever and ever
Every little thing that you do
Oh, every little thing that you do
Baby I'm amazed by you!
-Lonestar

I approached a child and asked, "What is love?"
The child answered "Love is when a puppy licks
your face. Even after you left him alone all day.
I want to be in a relationship where you telling
me you love me is just a ceremonious validation
of what you already show me.
=Steve Maraboli,
Life, the Truth, and Being Free

Love builds bridges where there are none.

Being deeply loved by someone gives you strength, while loving someone deeply gives you courage.
-Laozi

You brought the colors in my life!

Love is when you look into someone's eyes and see everything you need.

Love is a smoke made with the fumes of sighs.
-William Shakespeare

Love one another, but make not a bond of love. Let it rather be a moving sea between the shores of your soul.

Loved you yesterday
Love you still
Always have
Always will

How many slams in an old screen door?
Depends how loud you shut it.
How many slices in a bread?
Depends how thin you cut it.
How much good inside a day?
Depends how good you live 'em.
How much love inside a friend?
Depends how much you give 'em.
-Shel Silverstein

Just because someone doesn't love you the way you want them to, doesn't mean they don't love you with everything they have.

And now these three remain: faith, hope and love. But the greatest of these is love.
-The Holy Bible

Love has no age, no limit:
and no death.

I will stop loving you when an apple grows on a mango tree, on the 30th day of February.

There is never a time or place for true love. It happens accidentally, in a heartbeat, in a single flashing, throbbing moment.
-Sarah Dessen,
The Truth about Forever

Because of you I have found a whole new meaning of the word love.

When it comes down to it, you can like a face or
a body, but you don't fall in love with it.
You fall in love with the mind.
The way a person things, the way a person talks.
Beauty can attract people,
but your thoughts are what is going to make
them stay.

True love is not about
the hugs and kisses,
the "I love you's" or
the "I miss you's"
but about the chills that hit every part of your
spine when you think about him.

In those whom I like, I can find no common
denominator, in those whom I love I can: they
all make me laugh.
-W.H. Auden

Love is like a mountain – hard to climb, but
once you get to the top the view is beautiful.

A friend is someone who knows all about you
and still loves you.
-Elbert Hubbard

I fell in love the way you fall asleep;
slowly, and then all at once.
-John Green,
The Fault in our Stars

Only fools fall in love,
and I guess I am one of them.

Love is that condition in which the happiness of
another person is essential to your own.
-Robert A. Heinlein,
Stranger in a Strange Land

You are my best friend as well as my lover, and
I do not know which side of you I enjoy the
most.
I treasure each side,
just as I have treasured our life together.
-Nicholas Sparks,
The Notebook

So it's not gonna be easy.
It's going to be really hard;
we're gonna have to work at this every day, but I
want to do that because I want you.
I want all of you, forever, every day.
You and me . . . every day.
-Nicholas Sparks,
The Notebook

You don't love someone because they're perfect,
you love them in spite of the fact that they are
not.
-Jodi Picoult,
My Sister's Keepeer

Love isn't all about flirting, hugs, kisses and sex.
Love is about having the ability to take all those
things away and still having feelings for that
person.

If I had a flower for every time I thought of you,
I could walk through my garden forever.
-Alfred Tennyson

When someone loves you, the way they say your name is different. You know that your name is safe in their mouth.
-Jess C. Scott,
The Intern

Love doesn't make the world go round. Love makes the ride worthwhile.

We love the things we love for what they are.
-Robert Frost

"Some people don't understand the promises
they're making when they make them," I said.
"Right, of course. But you keep the promise
anyway. That's what love is.
Love is keeping the promise anyway."
-John Green,
The Fault in Our Stars

What I want is to be needed.
What I need is to be indispensable to somebody.
Who I need is somebody that will eat up all my
free time, my ego, my attention.
Somebody addicted to me.
A mutual addiction.
-Chuck Palahniuk.
Choke

Where there is love there is life.
-Mahatma Gandhi

If you want to know where your heart is, look
where your mind goes when it wonders.

Once upon a time there was a boy who loved a
girl, and her laughter was a question he wanted
to spend his whole life answering.
-Nicole Krauss,
The History of Love.

So, I love you because the entire universe
conspired to help me find you.
-Paulo Coelho,
The Alchemist

When your heart speaks, take good notes!

Every heart sings a song, incomplete, until
another heart whispers back. Those who wish to
sing always find a song. At the touch of a lover,
everyone becomes a poet.
-Plato

I love you also means I love you more
than anyone loves you,
or has loved you,
or will love you,
and also,
I love you in a way that no one loves you,
or has loved you,
or will love you,
and also,
I love you in a way that I love no one else,
and never have loved anyone else,
and never will love anyone else.
-Jonathan Safran Foer

The truth is that the more intimately you know someone, the more clearly you'll see their flaws. That's just the way it is. This is why marriages fail, why children are abandoned, why friendships don't last. You might think you love someone until you see the way the act when they're out of money or under pressure or hungry, for goodness' sake. Love is something different. Love is choosing to serve someone and be with someone in spite of their filthy heart. Love is patient and kind, love is deliberate. Love is hard. Love is pain and sacrifice, it's seeing the darkness in another person and defying the impulse to jump ship.

Absence is to love what wind is to fire; it
extinguishes the small, it rekindles the great.
-Comte Roger de Bussy-Rabutin

And I promise you this: No matter who enters
your life, I will love you more than any of them.

What's meant to be will always find a way!
-Trisha Yearwood

When we love, we always strive to become better than we are. When we strive to become better than we are, everything around us becomes better too.
-Paulo Coelho,
The Alchemist

You are the first and last thought on of my every day.

You decorated my life. Created a world where dreams are a part.
-Kenny Rogers

Doubt thou the stars are fire;
Doubt that the sun doth move;
Doubt truth to be a liar;
But never doubt I love."
-William Shakespeare,
Hamlet

Love is absolute loyalty.
People fade, looks fade, but loyalty never fades.
You can depend so much on certain people;
you can set your watch by them, and
that's love,
even if it doesn't seem very exciting.
-Sylvester Stallone

Love doesn't just sit there, like a stone, it has to be made, like bread; remade all the time, made new.
-Ursula K. Le Guin,
The Lathe of Heaven

I feel in love with you because of a million things you never knew you were doing.

The deepest principle in human nature is the craving to be appreciated.
-William James

You are the answer to every prayer I've offered.
You are a song, a dream, a whisper, and I don't
know how I could have lived without you for as
long as I have.
-Nicholas Sparks,
The Notebook

I can talk to hundreds of people in one day, but
none of them compare to the smile you can give
me in one minute.

I loved with a love that was more than love.
-Edgar Allan Poe

It is a curious thought,
but it is only when you see people looking
ridiculous
that you realize just how much you love them.
-Agatha Christie,
An Autobiography

And, in the end
the love you take
is equal to the love you make.
-Paul McCartney,
The Beatles Illustrated Lyrics

Love is an irresistible desire to be irresistibly
desired.
-Robert Frost

It takes you no time to fall in love, but it takes
years to know what love is.

I love you like a fat kid loves cake!
-Scott Adams

You know, when it works, love is pretty
amazing. It's not overrated. There's a reason for
all those songs.
-Sarah Dessen,
This Lullaby

Love endures all things!
-The Holy Bible

For the two of us, home isn't a place. It is a
person. And we are finally home.
-Stephanie Perkins,
Anna and the French Kiss

I read once that the ancient Egyptians had fifty
words for sand.
The Eskimos had a hundred words for snow.
I wish I had a thousand words for love, but
all that comes to mind is the way you move
against me while you sleep and there are no
words for that.
-Brian Andreas,
Story People

Well, it seems to me that the best relationships
- the ones that last –
are frequently the ones that are rooted in
friendship. You know, one day you look at the
person and you see something more than you
did the night before.
Like a switch has been flicked somewhere.
And the person who was just a friend is...
suddenly the only person you can ever imagine
yourself with.
-Gillian Anderson

When love is not madness it is not love.
-Pedro Calderon de la Barca

You are my favorite work of art!

One love, one heart, one destiny.
-Bob Marley

It was love at first sight, at last sight, at ever and
ever sight.
-Vladimir Nabokov,
Lolita

Love who you heart wants, not what your eyes
want. Don't worry about what other say or
thing. This love is yours, not theirs.

Of all forms of caution, caution in love is
perhaps the most fatal to true happiness.
-Bertrand Russell,
The Conquest of Happiness

How do I love thee?
Let me count the ways.
I love thee to the depth and breadth and height
My soul can reach.
-Elizabeth Barrett Browning

The beginning of love is the will to let those we
love be perfectly themselves, the resolution not
to twist them to fit our own image.
If in loving them we do not love what they are,
but only their potential likeness to ourselves,
then we do not love them:
we only love the reflection of ourselves we find
in them.
-Thomas Merton,
No Man Is an Island

What Is Love? I have met in the streets a very poor young man who was in love. His hat was old, his coat worn, the water passed through his shoes and the stars through his soul.
-Victor Hugo

If love was a storybook, we'd meet on the very first page!

Love is not affectionate feeling, but a steady wish for the loved person's ultimate good as far as it can be obtained.
-C.S. Lewis

When you say "I love you," you are making a promise with someone else's heart. Try to honor it.

If you remember me, then I don't care if everyone else forgets.
-Haruki Murakami,
Kafka on the Shore

Forget all the reasons why it won't work and believe the one reason it will.

Love is a temporary madness, it erupts like volcanoes and then subsides. And when it subsides, you have to make a decision. You have to work out whether your roots have so entwined together that it is inconceivable that you should ever part. Because this is what love is. Love is not breathlessness, it is not excitement, it is not the promulgation of promises of eternal passion, it is not the desire to mate every second minute of the day, it is not lying awake at night imagining that he is kissing every cranny of your body. No, don't blush, I am telling you some truths. That is just being "in love", which any fool can do. Love itself is what is left over when being in love has burned away, and this is both an art and a fortunate accident.

-Louis de Bernières,
Captain Corelli's Mandolin

I cannot fix on the hour,
or the spot,
or the look or the words,
which laid the foundation.
It is too long ago.
I was in the middle before
I knew that I had begun."
-Jane Austen,
Pride and Prejudice

I want
to do with you what spring does with the cherry
trees.
-Pablo Neruda,
Twenty Love Poems and a Song of Despair

I tend to fall in love with the people that share
my sense of humor. Because nothing is better
than looking over at someone you love, and
know they're smiling for the exact same reasons.

The heart has its reasons which reason knows
not.
-Blaise Pascal

When you trip over love, it is easy to get up. But
when you fall in love, it is impossible to stand
again.
-Albert Einstein

Love is what you've been through with
somebody.
- James Thurber

Being with you never felt wrong. It's the one
thing I did right. You're the one thing I did
right.
-Becca Fitzpatrick,
Crescendo

Maybe...you'll fall in love with me all over
again."
"Hell," I said, "I love you enough now. What do
you want to do? Ruin me?"
"Yes. I want to ruin you."
"Good," I said. "That's what I want too."
-Ernest Hemingway,
A Farewell to Arms

I'm not sentimental -
I'm as romantic as you are.
The idea, you know,
is that the sentimental person thinks things will
last –
the romantic person has a desperate confidence
that they won't.
-F. Scott Fitzgerald,
This Side of Paradise

DEFINITION NOT FOUND
IN THE DICTIONARY
Not leaving: an act of trust and love,
often deciphered by children.
-Markus Zusak,
The Book Thief

There are only four words that are far better
than
"I love you."
Those words are
"I'm here to stay."

My wish is that you may be loved to the point of
madness.
-André Breton,
What is Surrealism?: Selected Writings

Love is . . . Being happy for the other person
when they are happy, Being sad for the person
when they are sad, Being together in good times,
And being together in bad times.
LOVE IS THE SOURCE OF STRENGTH.

Love is . . . Being honest with yourself at all
times, Being honest with the other person at all
times, Telling, listening, respecting the truth,
And never pretending.
LOVE IS THE SOURCE OF REALITY.

Love is . . . An understanding so complete that
you feel as if you are a part of the other person,
Accepting the other person just the way they
are, And not trying to change them to be
something else.
LOVE IS THE SOURCE OF UNITY.

Love is . . . The freedom to pursue your own
desires while sharing your experiences with the
other person, The growth of one individual
alongside of and together with the growth of
another individual.
LOVE IS THE SOURCE OF SUCCESS.

Love is . . . The excitement of planning things
together, The excitement of doing things
together.
LOVE IS THE SOURCE OF THE FUTURE.
Love is . . . The fury of the storm, The calm in
the rainbow.
LOVE IS THE SOURCE OF PASSION.

Love is . . . Giving and taking in a daily situation,
Being patient with each other's needs and
desires.
LOVE IS THE SOURCE OF SHARING.

Love is . . . Knowing that the other person will
always be with you regardless of what happens,
Missing the other person when they are away
but remaining near in heart at all times.
LOVE IS THE SOURCE OF SECURITY.
LOVE IS . . . THE SOURCE OF LIFE!"
-Susan Polis Schutz

Love has nothing to do with what you are
expecting to get - only with what you are
expecting to give - which is everything.
-Katharine Hepburn,
Me: Stories of My Life

I can't promise to fix all of your problems, but I
can promise you won't have to face them alone.

This is what we call love. When you are loved,
you can do anything in creation. When you are
loved, there's no need at all to understand what's
happening, because everything happens within
you.
-Paulo Coelho
The Alchemist

When I am with you, we stay up all night.
When you're not here, I can't go to sleep.
Praise God for those two insomnias!
And the difference between them."
-Rumi

Watch out for intellect,
because it knows so much it knows nothing
and leaves you hanging upside down,
mouthing knowledge as your heart
falls out of your mouth."
-Anne Sexton,
The Complete Poems

Ah, God, you sent him to me knowing that I would love him beyond reason.

Romance is the glamour which turns the dust of everyday life into a golden haze.
-Elinor Glyn

A thousand miles seem pretty far, but they've got planes, trains, and cars. I'd walk if I had no other way.

All I ever wanted was to reach out and touch
another human being not just with my hands
but with my heart.
-Tahereh Mafi,
Shatter Me

The best way to love is not to "fall" but to
"feel."

Who, being loved, is poor?"
-Oscar Wilde

Sometimes when I look at you, I feel I'm gazing
at a distant star.
It's dazzling, but the light is from tens of
thousands of years ago.
Maybe the star doesn't even exist anymore. Yet
sometimes that light seems more real to me than
anything.
-Haruki Murakami,
South of the Border, West of the Sun

I could not tell you if I loved you the first moment I saw you, or if it was the second or third or fourth. But I remember the first moment I looked at you walking toward me and realized that somehow the rest of the world seemed to vanish when I was with you.
-Cassandra Clare,
Clockwork Prince

Love does not consist of gazing at each other,
but in looking outward together in the same
direction.
-Antoine de Saint-Exupéry,
Airman's Odyssey

Breathe it all in. Love it all out.

If there ever was somebody who made me
believe in me, it was you.
-Garth Brooks

Love isn't when there are no fights in the relationship. Love is when once the fight ends, love is still there.

The highest function of love is that it makes the loved one a unique and irreplaceable being."
-Tom Robbins,
Jitterbug Perfume

Any person can say that they love you. Only a few will actually prove it.

When I say it's you I like, I'm talking about that
part of you that knows that life is far more than
anything you can ever see or hear or touch. That
deep part of you that allows you to stand for
those things without which humankind cannot
survive. Love that conquers hate, peace that
rises triumphant over war, and justice that
proves more powerful than greed.
-Fred Rogers

Love is a decision, it is a judgment, it is a
promise. If love were only a feeling, there would
be no basis for the promise to love each other
forever. A feeling comes and it may go. How
can I judge that it will stay forever, when my act
does not involve judgment and decision.

-Erich Fromm,
The Art of Loving

One word
Frees us of all the weight and pain of life:
That word is love.
-Sophocles

Love is simple.

You are the one girl that made me risk
everything for a future worth having.
-Simone Elkeles,
Perfect Chemistry

Love is the extremely difficult realization that something other than oneself is real.
-Iris Murdoch,
Existentialists and Mystics Writings on Philosophy and Literature

Love doesn't need to be perfect, it just needs to be true.

Trust your heart if the seas catch fire, live by love though the stars walk backward.
-E.E. Cummings

Friends can help each other. A true friend is someone who lets you have total freedom to be yourself - and especially to feel. Or, not feel. Whatever you happen to be feeling at the moment is fine with them. That's what real love amounts to - letting a person be what he really is.

-Jim Morrison

You don't love someone because of their looks
or their clothes or their car.
You love them because they sing a song only
your heart can understand.
-Oscar Wilde

Baby when it's love if it isn't rough it isn't fun.
-Lady Gaga,
Pokerface

To give pleasure to a single heart by a single
kind act is better than a thousand head-bowings
in prayer.
-Saadi

Love is not the absence of logic
but logic examined and recalculated
heated and curved to fit
inside the contours of the heart.
-Tammara Webber,
Easy

Come sleep with me: We won't make Love,
Love will make us.
-Julio Cortázar

You can have friendship and you can have love,
but it is only when you have both together that
it will be a great love.

If a thing loves, it is infinite.
-William Blake

Love does not begin and end the way we seem
to think it does.
Love is a battle, love is a war;
Love is a growing up.
-James A. Baldwin

Love is like a friendship caught on fire. In the
beginning a flame, very pretty, often hot and
fierce, but still only light and flickering. As love
grows older, our hearts mature and our love
becomes as coals, deep-burning and
unquenchable.
-Bruce Lee

I like flaws. I think they make things interesting.
-Sarah Dessen,
The Truth About Forever

Love is when you have 100 reasons to leave someone, but still you look for one reason to fight for them.

The world was collapsing, and the only thing that really mattered to me was that she was alive.
-Rick Riordan,
The Last Olympian

Keep love in your heart. A life without it is like a sunless garden when the flowers are dead.
-Oscar Wilde

Love is caring for each other even when you are angry.

Do all things with love.
-Og Mandino

Every long lost dream led me to where you are
Others who broke my heart they were like
Northern stars
Pointing me on my way into your loving arms
This much I know is true
That God blessed the broken road
That led me straight to you
-Rascal Flatts
The Broken Road

I'd do almost anything for love, within safe
boundaries. I've flown to places to surprise
people, even if it was just for a day. I think it's so
important to keep the romance alive and make
sure the fun and spontaneity are there.
-Brittany Murphy

A woman knows the face of the man she loves
as a sailor knows the open sea.
-Honore de Balzac

True love isn't found. It's built.

A man is already halfway in love with any
woman who listens to him.
-Brendan Francis

I have found the paradox, that if you love until it hurts, there can be no more hurt, only more love.
-Mother Teresa

Immature love says: 'I love you because I need you.' Mature love says 'I need you because I love you.'
-Erich Fromm

Affection is responsible for nine-tenths of whatever solid and durable happiness there is in our lives.
-C. S. Lewis

Romance is important, but to have a friend you can use as a mirror, who can give you an objective response, that's what's really important.
-Jake Gyllenhaal

Romance is sort of an island right next to care. When you care about someone and you listen to them and you hear them and you can feel them and you know just what's right, and generally it's something that will be very unimpressive to a room of strangers.
-Ashton Kutcher

Love is composed of a single soul inhabiting
two bodies.
-Aristotle

Falling in love is easy, staying in love requires
work.

I think great romance needs great obstacles and
textures.
-Ang Lee

Men always want to be a woman's first love -
women like to be a man's last romance.
-Oscar Wilde

You be the anchor that keeps my fee on the
ground. I will be the wings that keep your heart
in the clouds.

There is always some madness in love. But there
is also always some reason in madness.
-Friedrich Nietzsche

Experts on romance say for a happy marriage
there has to be more than a passionate love. For
a lasting union, they insist, there must be a
genuine liking for each other. Which, in my
book, is a good definition for friendship.
-Marilyn Monroe

I have been astonished that Men could die
Martyrs for religion.
I have shudder'd at it,
I shudder no more.
I could be martyr'd for my Religion.
Love is my religion.
I could die for that.
I could die for you.
- John Keats

Love me and the world is mine.
-David Reed

Every love story is beautiful, but our is my favorite.

You know you're in love when you don't want to fall asleep because reality is finally better than your dreams.
-Dr. Seuss

True love stories never have endings.
-Richard Bach

He held her like a seashell, and listened to her heart.

We love because it's the only true adventure.
-Nikki Giovanni

When you love someone,
they're a part of you.
It's like you're attached
by this invisible thread, and
no matter how far away you are,
you can always feel them.

The only thing that matters is what they feel,
and how much they feel, for each other.
And if it's half of what we felt
— that's everything.
-Guess Who's Coming to Dinner

Listen to me, Mister. You're my knight in
shining armor . . . and don't you forget it.
-Katherine Hepburn to Henry Fonda,
On Golden Pond

I like when you smile, but I love when I'm the
reason.

My Creed is Love and you are its only tenet.
-John Keats

I don't wish to be everything to everyone, but I would like to be something to someone.
-Javan

Love cannot be found where it doesn't exist, nor can it be hidden where it truly does.

Tell me who admires you and loves you, and I will tell you who you are.
-Charles Augustin Sainte-Beuve

To find someone who will love you for no
reason,
and to shower that person with reasons,
that is the ultimate happiness.
-Robert Brault

You and you alone make me feel that I am alive.
Other men it is said have seen angels,
but I have seen thee and thou art enough.
-George Moore

He felt now that he was not simply close to her,
but that he did not know where he ended and
she began.
-Leo Tolstoy,
Anna Karenina

True love begins when nothing is looked for in
return.

He who loves is a slave; he who is loved is the
master.
-Polish Proverb

All, everything that I understand, I understand
only because I love.
-Leo Tolstoy,
War and Peace

Wouldn't it be the perfect crime if I stole your
heart and you stole mine.

What we have once enjoyed we can never lose.
All that we love deeply becomes a part of us.
-Helen Keller

I love your feet
because they have
wandered over
the earth and through
the wind and water
until they brought
you to me.
-Pablo Neruda

We need a witness to our lives. There's a billion people on the planet... I mean, what does any one life really mean? But in a marriage, you're promising to care about everything. The good things, the bad things, the terrible things, the mundane things... all of it, all of the time, every day. You're saying 'Your life will not go unnoticed because I will notice it. Your life will not go un-witnessed because I will be your witness.

-Shall We Dance?

What will survive of us is love.
-Phillip Larkin,
An Arundel Tomb

No one else will ever know the strength of my love. For you're the only one who knows what my hear sounds like from the inside.

Love must be as much a light, as it is a flame.
-Henry David Thoreau

Love doesn't sit there like a stone, it has to be made, like bread; remade all of the time, made new.
-Ursula K. Le Guin

You are my sunshine my only sunshine. You make me happy when skies are gray!

We loved with a love that was more than love.
-Edgar Allan Poe,
Annabell Lee

The minute I heard my first love story
I started looking for you, not knowing
how blind that was.
Lovers don't finally meet somewhere.
They're in each other all along.
-The Essential Rumi

I love you, not only for what you are,
but for what I am when I am with you.
I love you, not only for what you have made of
yourself but for what you are making of me.
-Roy Croft

Better never to have met you in my dream than to wake and reach for hands that are not there.
-Otomo No Yakamochi

It's not being in love that makes me happy. It's being in love with you that makes me happy.

I love being married. It's so great to find that one special person you want to annoy for the rest of your life.
-Rita Radner

I love you. You annoy me more than I ever thought possible, but… I want to spend every irritating minute with you.
-*Scrubs*

Love is not a because. It's a no matter what.

If you live to be 100, I hope I live to be 100 minus one day, so I never have to live without you.
-Ernest H. Shephard

When you realize you want to spend the rest of
your life with somebody,
you want the rest of your life to start as soon as
possible.
-When Harry Met Sally

No. No, you can't… STOP. Please don't go away. Please? No one's ever stuck with me for so long before. And if you leave… if you leave… I just, I remember things better with you. I do, look. P. Sherman, forty-two… forty-two… I remember it, I do. It's there, I know it is, because when I look at you, I can feel it. And-and I look at you, and I… and I'm home. Please… I don't want that to go away. I don't want to forget.
-*Finding Nemo*

I love you right up to the moon — and back.
-Sam McBratney,
Guess How Much I Love You

Being someone's first love may be great, but to
be their last love is beyond perfect.

I would rather share one lifetime with you than
face all the ages of this world alone.
-The Fellowship of the Ring

Now join your hands, and with your hands your
hearts.
-William Shakespeare

The most memorable people in your life will be
the people who loved you when you weren't
lovable.

Where your treasure is, there will your heart be
also.
-*Harry Potter and the Deathly Hallows*
(and yes, Matthew 6:21, too)

You have made a place in my heart where I
thought there was no room for anything else.
You have made flowers grow where I cultivated
dust and stones.
-Robert Jordan,
The Wheel of Time

It's still the same old story
A fight for love and glory
A case of do or die
The world will always welcome lovers
As time goes by.
-"*As Time Goes By*"
from *Casablanca*
by Dooley Wilson

Distance is a test to see how far love can travel.

Happiness is anyone and anything at all, that's loved by you.
-You're A Good Man, Charlie Brown

Love is sweet when it is new, but it is sweeter when it is true.

It was a million tiny little things that, when you added them all up, the meant we were suppose to be together. . . and I knew it.
-Sleepless in Seattle

This is the start of your sweet little story. The part where your page meets mine. No matter where your tale takes you tomorrow, our story will always be read – Love.

Love means never having to say you're sorry.
-Jennifer Cavalleri,
Love Story

Don't know much about history
Don't know much biology
Don't know much about a science book
Don't know much about the French I took

But I do know that I love you
And I know that if you love me too
What a wonderful world this would be!
-Wonderful World
by Sam Cooke

In the end,
you'll know which people really love you.
They're the ones who see you
for who you are, and
no matter what,
always find a way
to be at your side.

One is very crazy when in love.
-Sigmund Freud

When a girl is in love you can see it in her smile.
When a guy is in love you see it in his eyes.

Forever isn't log as long as I am with you.
-Winne the Pooh

The best part of the day is when you and me
become we!

We come to love not by finding a perfect
person, but by learning to see the imperfect
person perfectly.
-Sam Keen

You are the ketchup to my fries.

L is for the way you look at me
O is for the only one I see
V is very, very extraordinary
E is even more than anyone that you adore

You get mad sometimes
I drive you right out of your mind
I don't mean to make you crazy
I'm not the devil just a dude
Baby girl I know that you
Could do better than me maybe
But it's too late, you already love me
-Toby Keith

Love is watching someone else's boring show on
TV

The only present love demands is love.
-John Gay

And you bravely tied your life to mine and we
set sail toward forever under the moonless sky.

I love you not only for what you are but for
what I am when I am with you.

There is no greatness without passion.
-Tony Robbins

It's you. It's always been you

I wanna be the wind that fills your sails
And be the hand that lifts your veil
And be the moon that moves your tide
The sun coming up in your eyes
Be the wheels that never rust
And be the spark that lights you up
All that you've been dreaming of and more
So much more, I wanna be your everything
-Keith Urban

You may fall in love
with the beauty of someone,
but remember that finally
you have to live
with the character,
not the beauty.

We can't be wise and in love at the same time.
-Bob Dylan

Tell me the story about how the sun loved the moon so much he died every night to let her breathe.

When someone loves you, they don't always have to say it. You can always know it by the way they treat you.
-Carson Kalhoff

He's not the only guy in the universe, but he's the only one that matters.

My heart is, and always will be, yours.
-Sense and Sensibility

True love is friendship set on fire.

We tend to fall in love
the same way we get sick:
without wanting to,
without believing it,
against our will.

Love isn't when you can name
a million things you love about the person.
Love is when you can't even find
the words to describe
how you feel about them.

You are my sun, my moon, and all of my stars.

When I felt my feet slipping, you came with
your love and kept me steady.
-Psalm 94:18

You fall in love with the most unexpected
person at the most unexpected time.

A simple "I love you" means more than money.
-Frank Sinatra

Love is falling asleep on the couch and waking
up with blanket on you.

I like to believe that love is a reciprocal thing,
that it can't really be felt truly, by one.
-Sean Penn

Love is a meeting of two souls,
fully accepting the dark and light
within each other
bound by the courage
to grow thru struggle
into bliss.

The say,
"A picture is worth a thousand words."
But I think they are wrong
when I looked at yours,
I was speechless.

Love to me is someone telling me,
"I want to be with you for the rest of my life,
and if you needed me to I'd jump out of a plane
for you."
-Jennifer Lopez

Familiar acts are beautiful through love.
-Percy Shelley

To be brave is to love unconditionally without
expecting anything in return.
-Madonna

There are all kinds of love in the world, but
never the same love twice.
-F. Scott Fitzgerald.

Anyone can love a rose, but it takes a great deal
to love a leaf. It's ordinary to love the beautiful,
but it is beautiful to love the ordinary.

When love is real it finds a way.
-Avatar Roku

Roses are read
Violets are blue
When things fall apart
Love is the glue

Lust is temporary, romance can be nice, but love is the most important thing of all. Because without love, lust and romance will always be short-lived.
-Danielle Steel

I am a better person when I let myself have the
time for romance and for love.
-Diane Kruger

You are like bacon. You make everything
better.

Romance is tempestuous. Love is calm.
-Mason Cooley

Hatred paralyzes live; love releases it.
Hatred confuses life; love harmonizes it.
Hatred darkens life; love illumines it.
-Martin Luther King, Jr.

IN THE END

ALWAYS CHOOSE LOVE!

www.ingramcontent.com/pod-product-compliance
Lightning Source LLC
Chambersburg PA
CBHW050119280326
41933CB00010B/1170